Crochet your CHRISTMAS BAUBLES

25 Christmas Decorations to Make

DAVID & CHARLES

www.davidandcharles.com

Contents

Introduction

Crochet your own fun and festive collection of Christmas tree decorations from these 25 simple-to-crochet patterns in five seasonal themes.

Enter Santa's Grotto and meet Santa Claus, Nordic Elf, Rudolph the Red-nosed Reindeer and a string of dancing Gingerbread Men. Then you need as many cute amigurumi beaded Christmas trees as you can crochet to complete the Christmas magic!

Children and the young at heart will love the characters from Fairy Tales and Frozen Winter Wonderland. Guaranteed to brighten up your festivities, the quirky characters and bold decorations are sure to become family favourites, creating Christmas memories to treasure.

If you are looking for something more sophisticated, add some traditional baubles from the White Christmas collection or try some easy-to-crochet Scandinavian Style baubles in classic red and vintage white. The patterns for matching bunting will complete the festive fun!

The patterns are all quick and easy-to-follow and make perfect decorations for your own home or to crochet as gifts for family and friends, so pick up your hook and crochet some Christmas cheer.

Santa's Grotto

Designed by Cara Medus

Welcome to Santa's Grotto, featuring Santa Claus, his extra special reindeer, Rudolf, the original Nordic elf, Bushy Evergreen, and a string of dancing gingerbread men. The final project, a beaded Christmas tree, completes the collection in style. The patterns are worked using the amigurumi method: crochet as many as you like to add character and charm to your tree.

Santa's Grotto

Santa Claus

FINISHED MEASUREMENTS

12cm (4⅜in) tall

YOU WILL NEED

DMC Natura Just Cotton yarn (100% cotton, 50g/155m per ball):

A 50g (1¾oz) of shade N11 Noir

B 50g (1¾oz) of shade N23 Passion

C 50g (1¾oz) of shade N01 Ibiza

D 50g (1¾oz) of shade N35 Nacar

E oddments of shade N16 Tournesol

F oddments of shade N39 Ombre

Crochet hook: 2.5mm (US B/1 or C/2)

Tapestry needle

Embroidery needle

Toy stuffing

Pattern notes

These patterns are worked using the amigurumi method. Work stitches continuously in a spiral without closing off each round with a slip stitch unless directed otherwise. It may help to use a stitch marker in the first stitch of each round, moving it up as you work. When changing colour, pick up the new colour in the last yrh of the previous stitch. When fastening off, leave tails of yarn that can be used for sewing the pieces together afterwards, unless instructed to weave in ends.

Start here

Legs (make 2)

Using A, make a magic ring.
Round 1 (RS): Ch1 (does not count as st), 6dc into the ring. [6 sts]
Round 2: 2dc into each st around. [12 sts]
Rounds 3–5: Dc in each st around. Change to B.
Rounds 6–10: Using B, dc in each st around. Fasten off on first leg only. Make second leg, don't fasten off.

Joining the legs

When you have finished the second leg, work another 3dc on second leg, then beginning in the next unworked st on the first leg, 10dc. (This places the seams at the back of the legs.) The next st will be back on the second leg, but you will need to leave two stitches in the centre unworked before continuing on the second leg. Work 7dc on the second leg to complete the round.
Use the tail end from the first leg to sew together the two unworked sts in the centre of both legs.
You will now have a round of 20 sts. Do not fasten off.

Body

Round 1 (RS): 2dc in each st around. [40 sts]
Round 2: Dc in each st around.
Round 3: (4dc, dc2tog, 5dc, dc2tog) twice, (5dc, dc2tog) twice. [34 sts]
Round 4: Working in back loop only: (6dc, dc2tog, 7dc, dc2tog) twice. [30 sts]
Round 5: Working in both loops: (5dc, dc2tog, 6dc, dc2tog) twice. [26 sts]
Rounds 6–8: Dc in each st around.
Round 9: (11dc, dc2tog) twice. [24 sts]
Round 10: (2dc, dc2tog) 6 times. [18 sts]
Round 11: (7dc, dc2tog) twice. [16 sts]

Flatten the top ready to close straight across with a dc seam. Work enough sts to position the hook and yarn at one end of the seam, stuff and then dc through both layers to close. Fasten off and weave in ends.

Skirt

Rejoin B at centre back in one of the remaining loops from Round 3 of the body. Make sure the legs are facing away from you when you rejoin the yarn, so the RS of the work will show when you continue working in the round.
Round 1 (RS): Ch1 (does not count as st), dc in each st around, ss to first dc. [34 sts]
Rounds 2–4: Rep Round 1, change to C at the end of Round 4.
Round 5: Ch1 (does not count as st), (2dc in next st, 16dc) twice, ss to first dc. [36 sts]
Round 6: Ch1 (does not count as st), dc in each st around, ss to first dc.
Round 7: Working in front loop only: Ch1 (does not count as st), dc in each st around, ss to first dc.
Round 8: As Round 6, fasten off and weave in ends.

Arms (make 2)

Using D, make a magic ring.
Round 1 (RS): Ch1 (does not count as st), 4dc into ring. [4 sts]
Round 2: 2dc in each st around. [8 sts]
Rounds 3–4: Dc in each st around, change to B at the end of Round 4.
Round 5: Working in back loop only: dc in each st around.
Continue working in a spiral on these 8 sts until the arm measures 5cm (2in). Fasten off.
Rejoin C in remaining loops of Round 4 with hand facing away from you.
Next round: Ch1 (does not count as st), 4dc, 2dc in next st, 3dc, dc in same st as first dc, ss in next dc, fasten off and weave in ends.

Head

Using D, make a magic ring.
Round 1 (RS): Ch1 (does not count as st), 6dc into ring. [6 sts]
Round 2: 2dc in each st around. [12 sts]
Round 3: (2dc in next st, 1dc) 6 times. [18 sts]
Round 4: Dc in each st around.
Round 5: (2dc in next st, 5dc) 3 times. [21 sts]
Rounds 6–10: Dc in each st around.
Round 11: (5dc, dc2tog) 3 times. [18 sts]
Round 12: Dc in each st around.
Round 13: (1dc, dc2tog) 6 times. [12 sts]
Stuff the head.
Round 14: (Dc2tog) 6 times. Fasten off, using the tail to sew the remaining hole closed, and leave the tail for sewing to the body.

Hat

Using B, ch2.
Round 1 (RS): 4dc in second ch from hook. [4 sts]
Round 2: (2dc in next st, 1dc) twice. [6 sts]
Round 3: Dc in each st around.
Round 4: (2dc in next st, 2dc) twice. [8 sts]
Round 5: Dc in each st around.
Round 6: (2dc in next st, 3dc) twice. [10 sts]
Round 7: Dc in each st around.
Round 8: (2dc in next st, 4dc) twice. [12 sts]
Round 9: (2dc in next st, 5dc) twice. [14 sts]
Round 10: (2dc in next st, 6dc) twice. [16 sts]
Round 11: (2dc in next st, 7dc) twice. [18 sts]
Round 12: (2dc in next st, 5dc) 3 times. [21 sts]
Round 13: (2dc in next st, 6dc) 3 times. [24 sts]
Round 14: (2dc in next st, 7dc) 3 times. [27 sts]
Round 15: (2dc in next st, 8dc) 3 times. [30 sts]
Rounds 16--18: Dc in each st around, change to C at the end of

Round 18.
Round 19: (2dc in next st, 14dc) twice. [32 sts]
Round 20: Working in front loop only: dc in each st around.
Rounds 21–22: Dc in each st around. Ss into next st. Fasten off.

Hat bobble

Using C, ch2, leaving a long starting tail.
Round 1 (RS): 6dc in second ch from hook. [6 sts]
Round 2: 2dc in each st around. [12 sts]
Round 3: (Dc2tog) 6 times. [6 sts]
Fasten off, leaving a long tail. Stuff the bobble with starting tail of the yarn. Use finishing tail end to weave through remaining sts and pull together, then sew to the tip of the hat.

Beard

Using C, ch9.
Row 1 (WS): Dc in each st beginning with the second st from the hook, turn. [8 sts]
Row 2 (RS): Ch1 (does not count as st), dc in first st, 2dc in next st, dc in next 4 sts, 2dc in next st, dc in last st, turn. [10 sts]
Row 3: Ch1 (does not count as st), dc in first 2 sts, 2dc in next st, dc in next 4 sts, 2dc in next st, dc in last 2 sts, turn. [12 sts]
Row 4: Ch1 (does not count as st), skip first st, dc in next 2 sts, 2dc in next st, dc in next st, 2dc in each of next 2 sts, dc in next st, 2dc in next st, dc in next 2 sts, ss in next st, turn. [15 sts]
Row 5: Ch1 (does not count as st), skip ss and first dc, ss in next st, dc in next 10 sts, ss in next st, turn, leaving last st unworked. [12 sts]
Row 6: Ch1 (does not count as st), skip ss and first dc, ss in next st, dc in next 6 sts, ss in next st, do not turn or fasten off.

Beard edging

Work (ch-3 picot, ss into edge of beard) evenly around the lower edge and sides of the beard. When you reach the top edge, ss in each st across. At end of round, ss into st at base of first picot to join. Fasten off and weave in starting end.

Belt

Using A, ch34 and check that this chain will fit around Santa's waist; adjust by adding or removing ch. Ss to first ch to join into a ring, being careful not to twist.
Round 1 (RS): Ch1 (does not count as st), dc in each ch around, ss to first dc. Fasten off leaving a long tail. Weave in starting tail.
Sew the belt around Santa's waist at the join of the skirt.
Take a strand of E and split it in half. Embroider a belt buckle onto the front of the belt, using the photograph as a guide.

Making up and finishing

Pin and sew all pieces together. Take a length of F, and split it so that you are using two strands of the cotton. Take approximately 1m (40in) of B and use it to sew the tip to the back of the hat. Pass the end of this length through to the top of the hat, and make a slip knot as close as possible to the hat. Put the hook into the slip knot and ss back into the top of the hat at the point where the thread emerges. Ch40 and ss back into the hat for a hanger. Fasten off and weave in end underneath the fold of the hat at the back.

Rudolph the Reindeer

Start here

Legs (make 2)

Work as for the legs on Santa Claus, using A for the first 5 rounds and changing to B for the next 5 rounds. Complete the joining round as for Santa Claus; do not fasten off. [20 sts]

Body

Round 1 (RS): 9dc, 2dc in each of next 8 sts (across the front of the reindeer), 3dc. [28 sts]
Round 2: Dc in each st around.
Round 3: 9dc, dc2tog, 12dc, dc2tog, 3dc. [26 sts]
Round 4: 9dc, dc2tog, 10dc, dc2tog, 3dc. [24 sts]
Round 5: 9dc, dc2tog, 8dc, dc2tog, 3dc. [22 sts]
Round 6: 11dc, dc2tog, 4dc, dc2tog, 3dc. [20 sts]
Round 7: 11dc, dc2tog, 2dc, dc2tog, 3dc. [18 sts]
Rounds 8–9: Dc in each st around.
Round 10: (Dc2tog, 7dc) twice. [16 sts]
Round 11: Dc in each st around, finish the body as for Santa Claus, leaving a tail for sewing the head to the body.

Arms (make 2)

Using A, make a magic ring.
Round 1 (RS): Ch1 (does not count as st), 7dc into the ring. [7 sts]
Rounds 2–4: Dc in each st around, change to B at the end of Round 4. Continue working in a spiral on these 7 sts until the arm measures 5cm (2in). Fasten off. Sew the arms to the body.

Head (worked from bottom to top)

Using B, make a magic ring.
Round 1: Ch1 (does not count as st), 6dc into the ring. [6 sts]
Round 2: 2dc in each st around. [12 sts]
Round 3: (2dc in next st, 1dc) 6 times. [18 sts]
Round 4: Dc in each st around.
Round 5: (2dc in next st, 5dc) 3 times. [21 sts]
Rounds 3–5: Dc in each st around.
Round 6: (5dc, dc2tog) 3 times. [18 sts]
Round 7: Dc in each st around.
Round 8: (4dc, dc2tog) 3 times. [15 sts]
Round 9: Dc in each st around.
Round 10: (2dc in next st, 4dc) 3 times. [18 sts]
Round 11: Dc in each st around.
Round 12: (1dc, dc2tog) 6 times. [12 sts]
Stuff the head.
Round 13: (2dc, dc2tog) 3 times; do not fasten off. [9 sts]

Ears

*Ch3, htr in second ch from hook, dc in next ch, dc in st at base of ch**.
If you only start with 3 ch, and you htr in the second ch from hook, then dc in the next ch, there isn't another chain in which to do this dc. Either you start with 3ch or do 2dc in the first ch you made.
Flatten seam at top of head and ss across through both layers to close seam. For the second ear, rep from * to **, fasten off and weave in ends. Position the head in front of the body so that the top of the body is level approximately with Round 8 of the head. Use the tail end from the body to sew the head in place across the top of the body. Pass the yarn through the head to the front, to sew the bottom of the head to the chest, fasten off and weave in ends.

Scarf

Using C, ch4, leaving a long starting tail.
Row 1 (RS): Dc in second ch from hook and in next 2 ch, turn. [3 sts]
Row 2: Ch1 (does not count as st), dc in each st to end, turn.
Repeat Row 2 until the scarf measures 16cm (6¼in). Fasten off, leaving a long tail.
Using D, backstitch a stripe every two rows along the length of the scarf. Repeat with E for the alternate rows. Sew the scarf in place using the starting and finishing ends.

Nose

Using D, ch4.
Round 1: Dc in second ch from hook, dc in next ch, 4dc in next ch, working in the other side of the foundation ch, dc in next ch, 3dc in last ch, ss to first ch. Fasten off, leaving a long tail for sewing the nose to the head.

Antlers

First antler

Using A, (ch6, dc in second ch from hook and in next 2 ch) twice, ss in next ch, ch4, dc in second ch from hook and in next 2 ch, ss in same st as previous ss, dc in next unworked ch, ss in base of third dc worked (at base of first 'branch'), dc in each of 2 remaining unworked ch. Do not fasten off. Refer to diagram below.

Second antler

Ch8, dc in second ch from hook and in next 2 ch, ss in next ch, ch4, dc in second ch from hook and in next 2 ch, ss in same st as previous ss, dc in next unworked ch, ch4, dc in second ch from hook and in next 2 ch, ss in third ch of second antler (at base of first 'branch' of second antler), dc in each of 2 remaining unworked ch. Fasten off, leaving a long tail for sewing the antlers to the head, between the ears. Refer to diagram below.

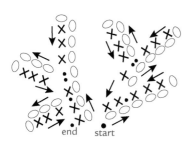

end   start

Making up and finishing

Using two strands of F, embroider the eyes and a mouth. Using B, ss to the top of the head, between the ears and behind the antlers. Ch40, ss back into the hat at the base of the ch to make a hanger. Fasten off and weave in ends.

Nordic Elf

FINISHED MEASUREMENTS

15cm (6in) tall

YOU WILL NEED

DMC Natura Just Cotton (100% cotton, 50g/155m per ball):

A 50g (1¾oz) of shade N11 Noir

B 50g (1¾oz) of shade N23 Passion

C 50g (1¾oz) of shade N01 Ibiza

D 50g (1¾oz) of shade N35 Nacar

E 50g (1¾oz) of shade N13 Pistache

F Oddments of shade N16 Tournesol

G Oddments of shade N39 Ombre

Crochet hook: 2.5mm (US B/1 or C/2)

Tapestry needle

Embroidery needle

Toy stuffing

Pink colouring pencil

Legs (make 2)

Work as for the legs on Santa Claus, using A for the first 5 rounds, and then alternating between 1 round of B and 1 round of C for the next 5 rounds. When joining the legs, work the next 3dc in C and continue the joining round of 20 sts in C.

Body

Work as for the body of Santa Claus, continuing to alternate between B and C for the first 2 rounds of the body and then change to E. Continue as for Santa Claus' body with E until end.

Skirt

Rejoin E at back in remaining loop of Round 3 of the body with the legs facing away from you.

Rounds 1–2 (RS): Ch1 (does not count as st), dc in each st around, ss to first dc. [34 sts]

Round 3: Ch1 (does not count as st), (2dc in next st, 16dc) twice, ss to first dc. [36 sts]

Round 4: *Dc in next st (the stitch after the ss), htr in next st, (tr, ch-2 picot, tr) in next st, htr in next st, dc in next st, ss in next st; rep from * 5 more times. Fasten off and weave in ends.

Arms (make 2)

Work as for Santa Claus, using E instead of B.

Head and belt

Work as for Santa Claus.

Collar

Using B, ch21.

Row 1 (RS): Dc in second ch from hook and in each ch to end, turn. [20 sts]

Row 2: Ch1 (does not count as st), (3dc, 2dc in next st) 5 times, turn. [25 sts]

Row 3: Ss in first st, *(dc, htr) in next st, (tr, ch-2 picot, tr) in next st, (htr, dc) in next st, ss in next st; rep from * 5 more times. Fasten off. [6 points]

Hat and bobble

Work as for Santa Claus, using E instead of B.

Ears

Left ear

Using D, ch2.

Round 1 (RS): 6dc in second ch from hook, ss to first dc.

Round 2: (Dc, htr, tr) in next st, ch-2 picot, ch3, ss in st at base of tr. Fasten off.

Right ear

Using D, ch2.

Round 1 (RS): 6dc in second ch from hook, ss to first dc.

Round 2: Ch3, ch-2 picot, (tr, htr, dc) in same st as ss, ss into next st. Fasten off.

Position the hat onto the head and sew the ears in place at either side, sewing through the hat and tucking the ears inside the brim.

Making up and finishing

Pin and sew all remaining pieces together. Using two strands of G, embroider the hair, eyes and mouth. Colour the cheeks with the pink colouring pencil. Using E, ss to the hat at the top of the head. Ch40, ss back into the hat at the base of the ch to make a hanger. Fasten off and weave in ends.

· ·

Beaded Christmas Tree

FINISHED MEASUREMENTS

13cm (5¼in) tall

YOU WILL NEED

DMC Natura Just Cotton (100% cotton, 50g/155m per ball):

A 50g (1¾oz) of shade N13 Pistache

B Oddments of shade N16 Tournesol

C Oddments of shade N39 Ombre

Crochet hook: 2.5mm (US B/1 or C/2)

Coloured wooden beads (approx. 20)

Tapestry needle

Toy stuffing

Craft glue

Start here

Tree

Using A, ch2.

Round 1 (RS): 4dc in second ch from hook.

Working in back loop only for the rest of the tree section:

Round 2: (2dc in next st, 1dc) twice. [6 sts]

Round 3: Dc in each st around.

Round 4: (2dc in next st, 2dc) twice. [8 sts]

Round 5: Dc in each st around.

Round 6: (2dc in next st, 3dc) twice. [10 sts]

Round 7: Dc in each st around.

Continue following this pattern of increasing 2 sts evenly in one round, and then working a plain round in the next round, until you have worked a total of 27 rounds and there are 30 sts. Fasten off and weave in ends.

Leaves

Each round of leaves is worked into the remaining loops that are visible around the tree. Work with the bottom of the tree facing away from you, starting at the bottom of the tree and working up. The first round of leaves is worked in the first round of loops at the bottom of the tree. You will then skip 2 rounds of loops and work the next round of leaves in the next round of loops. This continues all the way up the tree, skipping two rounds of loops between each round of leaves, until a total of 8 rounds of leaves have been worked.

Rounds 1 and 2:

Rejoin A into the first remaining loop of the round.

Leaf 1

Row1 (RS): Ch1 (does not count as st), dc in same st, dc in next 2 sts, turn. [3 sts]

Row 2: Ch1 (does not count as st), 3dc, turn.

Row 3: Skip first st, 5htr in next st, ss in next st, 2ss down side of leaf towards base, ss in base of third st of first row, ss in next st.

Repeat Rounds 1–3 for each leaf until

you have worked around the tree. Fasten off and weave in ends. It does not matter if the stitches of the round do not fit exactly into the stitch count of the round. You can either stop one stitch short of the starting point and ss in that stitch, or continue to make another leaf that will overlap the starting point of the round slightly. As the stitches continue in a spiral you can continue to work beyond the starting point of the round.

Once you have completed one round, fasten off, skip the next 2 rounds of loops and rejoin the yarn in the next round of loops. Repeat the above to make a second round of leaves.

Rounds 3 and 4:

Skip 2 rounds of loops, rejoin yarn in next round of loops.

Leaf 2

Row 1: Ch1 (does not count as st), dc in same st, dc in next 2 sts, turn. [3 sts]

Row 2: Skip first st, ss in each of next 2 sts, turn. [2 ss]

Row 3: 5htr in centre st of Row 1, ss in base of third st of first row, ss in next st.

Repeat Rows 1–3 around for each leaf. Fasten off and weave in ends. Sk next 2 rounds of loops and repeat round again. Fasten off and weave in ends.

Sk 2 rounds of loops, rejoin yarn in next round of loops.

Round 5: *(Ss, dc, htr, tr) in next st, (tr, htr, dc, ss) in next st; rep from * around. Fasten off and weave in ends. Sk 2 rounds of loops, rejoin yarn in next round of loops.

Round 6: *(Ss, dc, htr) in next st, (htr, dc, ss) in next st; rep from * around. Fasten off and weave in ends. Sk 2 rounds of loops, rejoin yarn in next round of loops.

Round 7: (Ch-3 picot, ss in next st) repeat around. Fasten off and weave in ends.

Sk 2 rounds of loops, rejoin yarn in next round of loops.

Round 8: (Ch-2 picot, ss in next st) repeat around. Fasten off and weave in ends.

Star

Using B, make a magic ring.

Round 1 (RS): Ch1 (does not count as st), 5dc into ring, ss to first dc. [5 sts]

Round 2: (Ch5, ss in next st) repeat around. Fasten off, leaving long tail. Use the tail of yarn to sew the star to the top of the tree.

Base

Using C, make a magic ring.

Round 1 (RS): Ch1 (does not count as st throughout), 6dc in the ring, ss to first dc. [6 sts]

Round 2: Ch1, 2dc in each st around, ss to first dc. [12 sts]

Round 3: Ch1, (1dc, 2dc in next st) 6 times, ss to first dc. [18 sts]

Round 4: Working in back loop only: dc in each st around, ss to first dc.

Rounds 5–6: Working in both loops: dc in each st around, ss to first dc, change to A at the end of round 6.

Round 7: Working in back loop only: ch1, (2dc, 2dc in next st) 6 times, ss to first dc. [24 sts]

Round 8: Working in both loops, ch1, (3dc, 2dc in next st) 6 times, ss to first dc. [30 sts]

In order to have the RS of the leaves at the top of the tree, you will need to insert the hook through the remaining loop top downwards, with the top of the tree towards you and the base of the tree facing away.

Stuff the tree and base. Join the tree and base by working a dc in each st of both layers around the bottom of the tree and base. Fasten off and weave in ends.

Making up and finishing

Using A, ss to the top of the tree behind the star. Ch40, ss back into the top of the tree at the base of the ch to make a hanger. Fasten off and weave in ends. Glue wooden beads to the leaves.

• •

Dancing Gingerbread Bunting

FINISHED MEASUREMENTS

Each gingerbread man:

10.5cm (4in) tall

Length of bunting with seven gingerbread men:

110cm (43in) wide

YOU WILL NEED

DMC Natura Just Cotton (100% cotton, 50g/155m per ball):

A 50g (1¾oz) of shade N37 Canelle (see Pattern notes)

B 50g (1¾oz) of shade N01 Ibiza

C Oddments of N13 Pistache

D Oddments of N23 Passion

E Oddments of N06 Rose Layette

F Oddments of N11 Noir

Crochet hook: 2.5mm (US B/1 or C/2)

Tapestry needle

Embroidery needle

8mm (⁵⁄₁₆in) buttons (approx.14)

Craft glue

Pattern notes

One ball of Canelle comfortably makes six gingerbread men, and is just enough for seven. However, depending on your tension, you may need two balls to complete all seven gingerbread men. The gingerbread motifs are worked in rounds for the head, then in rows from the head for the body and arms. For this pattern, each round is closed with a ss. You

will need to turn the work after each round of the head to make it appear consistent with the body, which is turned after every row. Where a dc2tog occurs at the beginning of a row, there is no turning ch, as this makes a neater stitch.

Gingerbread men (make 7)

Start here

Head

Using A, make a magic ring.

Round 1 (WS): Ch1 (does not count as st throughout), 6dc into the ring, ss to first dc, turn. [6 sts]

Round 2 (RS): Ch1, 2dc in each st around, turn. [12 sts]

Round 3: Ch1, (1dc, 2dc in next st) 6 times, ss to first dc, turn. [18 sts]

Round 4: Ch1, (2dc, 2dc in next st) 6 times, ss to first dc, turn. [24 sts]

Round 5: Ch1, (3dc, 2dc in next st) 6 times, ss to first dc, turn. [30 sts]

Round 6: Ss in first 3 sts, 3dc, 2dc in next st, 5dc, 2dc in next st, 3dc, ss in next 3 sts. (The following sts will form the first row of the body:) 3dc, 2dc in next st, 4dc, 2dc in next st, 2dc, ss to first st of round, turn. Do not fasten off.

Body (part 1)

Row 7: Ch1, 3dc, 2dc in next st, 5dc, 2dc in next st, 3dc, turn. [15 sts]

Row 8: Ch1, 3dc, 2dc in next st, 7dc, 2dc in next st, 3dc, turn. [17 sts]

Row 9: Ch1, 4dc, 2dc in next st, 7dc, 2dc in next st, 4dc, turn. Do not fasten off. [19 sts]

First arm

The first arm will be worked on the first 5 sts of the next row, then the yarn will be rejoined to work on the body over the next 9 sts.

Row 1 (RS): Ch1, 4dc, 2dc in next st, turn. [6 sts]

Row 2: Ch1, dc in each st to end, turn.

Row 3: Dc2tog, 3dc, 2dc in next st, turn. [6 sts]

Row 4: Ch1, dc in each st to end, turn.
Row 5: Dc2tog, 4dc, turn. [5 sts]
Row 6: Dc2tog, 1dc, dc2tog. Fasten off and weave in ends.

Body (part 2)

Rejoin A in the sixth stitch (marked stitch) of Row 9 of the body, with the RS facing.
Row 10 (RS): Ch1, 9dc, turn leaving remaining sts unworked. [9 sts]
Rows 11–12: Ch1, dc in each st to end, turn.
Row 13: Ch1, 2dc in first st, dc in each st to last st, 2dc in last st, turn. [11 sts]
Rows 14–16: Ch1, dc in each st to end, turn.
Row 17: Ch1, 2dc in first st, dc in each st to last st, 2dc in last st, turn. Do not fasten off. [13 sts]

First leg

The first leg will be worked over the first 7 sts of the next row, then the yarn will be rejoined in the seventh st (the same st as the end of the first leg) to work the second leg.
Row 1 (RS): Ch1, 5dc, dc2tog, turn. [6 sts]
Row 2: Ch1, dc in each st to end, turn.
Row 3: Ch1, 4dc, dc2tog, turn. [5 sts]
Row 4: Ch1, dc in each st to end, turn.
Row 5: Ch1, 3dc, dc2tog, turn. [4 sts]
Row 6: Dc2tog, 2dc. Fasten off and weave in ends.

Second leg

Rejoin A in the seventh stitch of Row 17 of the body with RS facing.
Row 1 (RS): Dc2tog, 5dc, turn. [6 sts]
Row 2: Ch1, dc in each st to end, turn.
Row 3: Dc2tog, 4dc, turn. [5 sts]
Row 4: Ch1, dc in each st to end, turn.
Row 5: Dc2tog, 3dc, turn. [4 sts]
Row 6: Ch1, 2dc, dc2tog, fasten off and weave in ends.

Second arm

There are 5 remaining unworked sts from Row 9 of the body; rejoin A in the first of these sts with RS facing.
Row 1 (RS): Ch1, 2dc in first st, 4dc, turn. [6 sts]
Row 2: Ch1, dc in each st to end, turn.
Row 3: Ch1, 2dc in first st, 3dc, dc2tog, turn. [6 sts]
Row 4: Ch1, dc in each st to end, turn.
Row 5: Ch1, 4dc, dc2tog, turn. [5 sts]
Row 6: Dc2tog, 1dc, dc2tog. Fasten off and weave in ends.

Edging

Rejoin A in the last stitch of the head, where it meets the body above the first arm. Dc evenly around the first arm, body, legs and second arm to where the head meets the body on the other side. Ss to the last st of the head to join. Underneath the arms and between the legs, ss into the point, and work extra dc on the external curves around the bottom of the arms and legs to avoid the edge pulling too tight. Fasten off and weave in ends.

White 'icing' border

Join B at the edge of the head in the last st just worked. Ss in each st around the entire edge of the motif, ss in first st to join. Fasten off leaving a long tail. Carry this tail across the back of the head to the right hand side of the mouth. Work 5 ss surface crochet stitches between Rounds 2 and 3 to form the mouth. Fasten off and weave in ends.

Bow tie

Choose either C, D or E, using the colours evenly across the motifs, ch10.
Row 1 (RS): Dc in second ch from the hook and in each ch to end, turn. [9 sts]
Row 2: Ch3 (counts as tr), tr in next st, htr in next st, dc in next 3 sts, htr in next st, tr in last 2 sts, turn.

In the following row, you will pinch the middle of the bow tie by working a dc stitch into the remaining loop of the foundation ch for the central 3 sts. Insert the hook into each of these 3 sts from back to front.
Row 3: Ch1 (does not count as st), dc in first 3 sts of Row 2, 3dc in central 3 sts of foundation ch, sk central 3 sts of Row 2, dc in each of last 3 sts of Row 2. Fasten off.

Making up and finishing

Sew the bow tie in place. With two strands of F, embroider French knots for eyes. The finished gingerbread men may benefit from spray blocking to help them lie perfectly flat; do this before you sew on the two buttons.

To make a hanging chain, with A, ch20, ss to first ch to join into a hanging loop. Ch20, *ss to end of the arm on the next motif, ch27 (or enough sts to make the chain long enough to reach across the back of the motif), ss into the end of the other arm on the motif, ch15. Rep from * until all motifs are joined, work further 5 ch so that there are 20 ch after the last motif, ch20 for hanging loop and ss into the 20th ch from the hook to join. Fasten off and weave ends back into the chain.

Frozen Winter Wonderland

Designed by Claire Wilson

Frozen Winter Wonderland features Belle the Icy Snow Princess, together with traditional snowflake baubles and snowmen with vintage hanging hearts and cute candy bows. The striking contrast between white, icy blue and silver shades and bright scarlet stripes makes this an enchanting theme for children and adults alike.

Frozen Winter Wonderland

Icy Snow Princess

Start here

Head

Using A, make a magic ring.
Round 1: Ch1, 5dc into the ring and tighten.
Round 2: 2dc in each st around. [10 sts]
Round 3: (2dc in next st, 1dc) around. [15 sts]
Round 4: (2c in next st, 2dc) around. [20 sts]
Round 5: (2dc in next st, 3dc) around. [25 sts]
Round 6: (2dc in next st, 4dc) around. [30 sts]
Rounds 7–10: Dc in each st around. Add the safety eyes (or buttons)

between Rounds 7 and 8. [30 sts]
Round 11: (Dc2tog, 4dc) around. [25 sts]
Round 12: (Dc2tog, 3dc) around. [20 sts]
Round 13: (Dc2tog, 2dc) around. [15 sts]
Round 14: (Dc2tog, 1dc) around. Fasten off. [10 sts]

Dress

Join B with a ss to the base of the head.
Round 1: Dc in each st around. [10 sts]
Round 2: 2dc in each stitch around. [20 sts]
Round 3: (2dc in next st, 1dc) around. [30 sts]
Round 4: Dc in each st around [30 sts]
Round 5: (3dc, dc2tog) around. [24 sts]
Rounds 6–8: Dc in each st around. [24 sts]
Round 9: (2dc in next st, 2dc) around. [32 sts]
Round 10: 2dc (2dc in next st, 2dc) around. [42 sts]
Rounds 11–12: Dc in each st around. [42 sts]
Round 13: (2dc in next st, 1dc) around. [63 sts]
Round 14: Dc in each st around. Ss to first dc of the round.

Hair

Using C, ch 15.
Rows 1–2: dc in each st. [15 sts]
Rows 3: 2dc in first st, dc along row, 2dc in last st. [17 sts]
Rows 4: 2dc in first st, dc along row, 2dc in last st. (19 sts).
Rows 5: 2dc in first st. dc along row, 2dc in last st. (21sts)
Rows 6: 3dc, 3tr, 2tr in next st, 2tr, sk1, dc, sk1, 2tr, 2tr in next st, 3tr, 3dc, Fasten off.
Repeat from * for other side of hair.

Making up and finishing

Stitch the hair to the top of the head with the straight edge facing the back.

To make the hanging loop, using D, ch30 and ss to first chain to form a loop. Sew to the top of the hair. If preferred, ch40 and fasten off.

Hang on the tree and then tie the ends in a bow around the top of the dress to decorate.

Cute Snowman

Start here

Snowman

Using A, ch6 and ss to first ch to form a ring. Use a stitch marker to mark the beginning of each round.
Round 1: 2dc in each st. [12 sts]

Round 2: (2dc in next st, 1dc) around. [18 sts]
Round 3: (2dc in next stitch, 2dc) around. [24 sts]
Rounds 4–7: Dc in each st around. [24 sts]
Round 8: (2dc in next st, 1dc) around. [36 sts]
Round 9: Dc in each st around. [36 sts]
Round 10: (Dc2tog, 2 dc) around. [27 sts]
Round 11: (Dc2tog, 1 dc) around. [18 sts]
Round 12: (Dc2tog, 1dc) around. [12 sts]
Round 13: (2dc in next stitch, 1dc) around. [18 sts]
Round 14: (2dc in next stitch, 2dc) around. [24 sts]
Rounds 15–16: Dc in each st around. Fit safety eyes (or sew on buttons) between rows 16 and 17. Stuff snowman.
Round 17: (Dc2tog, 2dc) around. [18 sts]
Round 18: (Dc2tog, 1dc) around. [12 sts]
Round 19: Dc2tog around [6 sts]
Round 20: Dc2tog around. [3 sts]
Fasten off and weave in ends to finish. Using D, sew a carrot nose.

Hat
Base
Using B, ch3 and ss to first st to form a ring. Use a stitch marker to mark the beginning of each round.
Round 1: 2dc in each st around. [6 sts]
Round 2:: 2dc in each st around. [12 sts]
Round 3: 2dc in each st around. [24 sts]
Round 4: (2dc in next stitch, 1dc) around. Ss to first st of round and fasten off. [36 sts]

Top
Using B, ch6 and ss to first ch to form a ring. Use a stitch marker to mark the beginning of each round.

Round 1: 2dc in each st around. [6 sts]
Round 2: 2dc in each st around. [12 sts]
Round 3: 2dc in each st around. [24 sts]
Round 4: Dc2tog around. [12 sts] Stuff and stitch to hat base.

Scarf
Using C, ch40. Work 3 rows of dc in each st. Fasten off. Make two small tassels of yarn and stitch to the ends of the scarf.

Making up and finishing
Using A, ch30. Ss to first ch to form a hanging loop and stitch to the top of the hat. Stitch the hat to the snowman body then stitch to scarf to the snowman body, crossing at the front.

● ● ● ● ● ● ● ● ● ● ● ● ● ● ● ● ●

Snowflake Bauble

FINISHED MEASUREMENTS
13cm (5¼in) circumference

YOU WILL NEED
Stylecraft Classique Cotton DK (100% cotton, 100g/184m per ball):
A 20g (¾ oz) of shade 3660 White

Oddments of shade 3667 Sky Blue
Crochet hook: 3mm (UK 11) (US D3)
Darning needle
Toy stuffing

Start here
Bauble
Using A, make a magic ring.
Round 1: Ch1, 5dc into the ring and tighten. [5 sts]
Round 2: 2dc in each of the next 4 st, 3dc in last st. [11 sts]
Round 3: 2dc in next st, 2dc. (2dc in next st, 1dc) 4 times. [16 sts]
Round 4: 2dc in next st, 3dc. (2dc in next st, 2dc) 4 times. [21 sts]
Round 5: 2dc in next st, 5dc. (2dc in next st, 4dc) 3 times. [25 sts]
Round 6: 2dc in next st, 8dc. (2dc in next st, 7dc) 2 times. [28 sts]
Round 7: 2dc in next st, 27dc. [29 sts]
Round 8: Dc in each st around. [29 sts]
Round 9: Dc2tog, 27dc. [28 sts]
Round 10: Dc2tog, 26dc. [27 sts]
Round 11: (Dc2tog, 7dc) around. [24 sts]
Round 12: (Dc2tog, 4dc) around. [20 sts]
Round 13: (Dc2tog, 2dc) around. [15 sts]
Round 14: (Dc2tog, 1dc) around. [10 sts]
Stuff firmly.
Round 15: Dc2tog around, leaving 5 sts. Fasten off, sew closed and sew in ends.

Snowflake detail
Using B, stitch a snowflake pattern on the front of the bauble. Stitch long lines first, make the diagonal lines slightly shorter than the horizontal and vertical, and stitch 'V' shapes at the end of each line.

Making up and finishing
Make the hanging cord using A. Ch20 and ss to first ch to form a loop. Stitch to the top of the bauble.

● ● ● ● ● ● ● ● ● ● ● ● ● ● ● ● ● ●

Doily Heart Hanger

FINISHED MEASUREMENTS

This will depend on the size of the card you choose

YOU WILL NEED

A Oddments of Rico Design Essentials Cotton Lurex in shade 001 White

Crochet hook: 3mm (UK 11) (US D3)

Old Christmas card / festive card stock

Glue

Scissors

Darning needle

Start here

Cut two cardboard heart shapes from the card stock in your desired size. Glue the hearts together with the wrong sides facing. Using a small hole punch or needle, make 33 evenly spaced holes around the heart, about 5mm (¼in) from the edge.
Round 1: Using the needle and a length of yarn, starting at the centre top of the heart, sew a blanket stitch around the edge of the heart using the holes you have made.
Round 2: Make 2dc in each sp made by the blanket stitch. Ss to first dc.
Round 3: Ch1, *3tr in next st, sk1, dc in next st. Repeat from * around, making an additional dc at the lowest point of the heart. Ss to first tr. Ch30. Ss to 1st ch to form a hanging loop.

• •

Candy Bow

FINISHED MEASUREMENTS

12cm (4 ⅜in) wide

YOU WILL NEED

Stylecraft Classique Cotton DK (100% cotton, 100g/184m per ball) in the following shades:

A 30g (1oz) of shade 3672 Poppy

B 30g (1oz) of shade 3660 White

Crochet hook: 4mm (UK 8, US G/6)

Darning needle

Start here

Main bow section

Using A, ch22
Rows 1–2: Ch1, dc in each st to end of row, turn. [22 sts]
Rows 3–4: Change to B. Ch1, dc in each st to end of row, turn. [22 sts]
Rows 5–12: Change to A. Repeat rows 1–4 twice more.
Rows 13–14: Change to A. Repeat rows 1–2.
Fasten off and weave in ends.

Middle bow section

Using A, ch4 +1 for turning ch.
Row 1: Dc in each st, turn. [4 sts]
Row 2: Ch1, dc in each st, turn. [4 sts]
Rows 3–12: Repeat Row 2.
Fasten off and leave a tail of around 25cm (10in) for sewing.

Making up and finishing

To make the hanging loop, using B, ch30 and ss to first ch to form a loop. Fold the main bow section into an accordion fold, pinching the middle into a bow shape. Secure temporarily with a sewing pin.

Take the middle bow section and wrap around the middle of the main bow section, removing the pin. Before stitching, catch the hanging cord in the middle bow section, to create the loop for hanging. Sew the ends of the middle bow section together.

Spray with starch if preferred.

• •

Fairy Tales

Designed by Anna Fazakerley

Children love fairy tales and this enchanting collection is sure to delight. Crochet the fancy festive fairy for the top of your tree, together with a jolly pair of Christmas birds: the tawny owl and red-breasted robin. They look great fun perched on the tree alongside beautifully crocheted red woodland toadstools or hanging out with the cheeky Scandi gnome.

Fairy Tales

Festive Fairy Princess

FINISHED MEASUREMENTS

19 cm (7½ in) tall

YOU WILL NEED

Oddments of Stylecraft Special DK yarn (100% Acrylic, 100g/295m per ball) in the following shades:

A Cream

B Candyfloss

C Fondant

D Wisteria

Additional yarn for hair: mix of weights and colours to theme with lilac shades

Crochet hook: 3mm (UK 11) (US D3)

Small safety eyes

Pink embroidery cotton (floss)

Yarn needle

Stitch marker

Toy stuffing

Cotton bud

Optional: glittery jewellery & beads

Head, Bottom half

Using A, make a magic ring.
Round 1: 6dc into the ring.
Round 2: 2dc in each st around. [12 sts]
Round 3: (Dc, 2dc in next st) around. [18 sts]
Round 4: (2dc, 2dc in next st) around. [24 sts]
Round 5: (3dc, 2dc in next st) around. [30 sts]
Round 6: (4dc, 2dc in next st) around. [36 sts]

Rounds 7--15: Dc into each st around.
Fasten off, leaving a long tail.

Top half

Using D, make a magic ring.
Repeat Rounds 1–9 as for the bottom half of the head.
Fasten off and sew in tail.
Place the eyes between Rounds 9 and 10 on the bottom half of the head, around 8 dc apart. Stuff the bottom half of the head and with the long tail, sew the bottom half to the top half, adding more stuffing to fill out when you are near the last few stitches.

Arms (make two)

Using A, make a magic ring.
Round 1: 8dc into the ring.
Rounds 2–14: Dc into each sts around.
Change to B.
Rounds 15–17: Dc into each st around. Fasten off, leaving a long tail. Stuff the hands only.

Legs (make two)

Using C, make a magic ring.
Round 1: 6dc into the ring.
Round 2: 2dc in each st around. [12 sts]
Round 3: (Dc, 2dc in next st) around. [18 sts]
Round 4: Bldc into each st around.
Round 5: Dc into each st around.
Round 6: 5dc, dc2tog for next 8 st, 5dc. [14 sts]
Round 7: 5dc, dc2tog for next 4 st, 5dc. [12 sts]
Change to A.
Round 8: Bldc into each st around.
Rounds 9–15: Dc into each st around [12 sts]. Fasten off and stuff.

Body

Join C to the top of the first leg where you fastened off.
Round 1: 2ch, line up the second leg so that the feet are pointing in the right direction, and dc into the stitch that is facing on the second leg. Then dc into each dc around the top of the second leg up to where you joined them, then work 2ch, then dc into the next st on the facing side of the first leg, next to where you joined the new colour, and dc into each st around the first leg to end. [28 sts]
Round 2: Dc into each st around including each ch.
Round 3: Dc into each st around.
Round 4: (5dc, dc2tog) around. Change to B.
Round 5: Bldc around.
Rounds 6–8: Dc into each st around.
Round 9: (2dc, dc2tog) around. [18 sts]
Rounds 10–15: Dc into each st around.
Fasten off, leaving a long tail and stuff leaving a little flex around the top of the legs if possible. Using C, sew up the gap between the 2ch spaces from Round 1.

Skirt

Turn the body upside down and join B to front loop in Round 5 of the body.
Round 1: Fldc around including the st where you joined the yarn. Join to first dc with ss.
Round 2: Ch3 (counts as tr), tr in same st, (2tr in next st) to end. Join with ss to top of ch3. [48 sts]
Round 3: Ch4 (counts as tr ch), tr in same st, sk next st. *(tr, ch1, tr) in next st, sk next st* repeat from *around. Join with ss to 3rd ch of beg ch 4. [48 tr, 24 ch1sp]
Change to C. Join in ch1 space of prev round.
Round 4: (Ch3, sk next 2 tr, ss into next ch1 sp) around. Fasten off and sew in tail.

Wings (make 2)

Round 1: Ch5, 5dtr in fifth ch from hook.
Round 2: Turn, ch4, dtr in same st, 2dtr in each st to end. [12 sts]
Round 3: Turn, ch6, ss in third ch from hook making picot, tr in same st, tr in next 6 st, htr in next 4 st, ss in last st. Fasten off, leaving a long tail.

Making up and finishing

Using long tails, stitch the arms to the sides of the body: hold the openings of the arms closed and oversew at the open edge of the body.

Using the long tail at the top of the body piece, position the head and stitch in place, stitching around twice for a solid join. Add a little more stuffing if needed, a few stitches from the end, to strengthen the neck area.

Wings

Hide the tail of one wing by stitching it in. Use the long tail of the other wing to stitch the wings together by the starting chains, with the picot stitches pointing downwards. They should look a little like butterfly wings. With the remainder of the long tail, stitch the wings to the centre of the back, about two rounds down from the base of the head.

Face

Embroider the mouth using pink embroidery cotton or thin yarn.

Hair

Choose some colourful yarns in various weights and shades. Wrap around your forearm between the hand and elbow to create lengths, then snip at the top and bottom of the loops to create hair strands. Attach each strand to the crown of the head by folding it in half, then hooking it through and looping the ends through the loop, as you would add a fringe to a scarf. Alternate different colours, then trim some to feather and layer the hair. Brush out the fibres, twisting the yarn to remove the plying and separate it out to appear like hair.

Wand

Strip the cotton wool from a cotton bud and wrap it from the top down with yarn. About 3cm (1¼in) from the end, thread the yarn onto a needle, push the cotton bud through the fary's hand and then thread the needle down the same way. Continue to wrap the yarn around the wand at the bottom.

Star

Using 4ply white glittery yarn and a 3mm crochet hook, make 3ch.
Round 1: 2ch, dc in 2nd ch from hook, (2ch, dc) 4 times, 2ch, slst to 1st dc.
Round 2: *slst in next ch sp, (3 ch, slst) 3 times in same ch sp, slst in next dc, * repeat between ** around. FO. (5 points with 3 x 3ch loops in each).

Tawny Owl

FINISHED MEASUREMENTS
10cm (4in) tall

YOU WILL NEED
Oddments of Stylecraft Special DK yarn (100% Acrylic, 100g/295m per ball) in the following shades:

A Meadow
B Plum
C Black
D Gold
E White
F Sunshine
G Spice
H Teal
Crochet hook: 3mm (UK 11) (US D3)
Yarn needle
Stitch marker
Toy stuffing

Start here

Body

Using A, make a magic ring
Round 1: 6dc into the ring.
Round 2: 2dc into each st around. [12 sts]
Round 3: (Dc in next dc, 2dc in next st) around. [18 sts]
Round 4: (2dc, 2dc in next st) around. [24 sts]
Round 5: (3dc, 2dc in next st) around. [30 sts]
Rounds 6–8: Dc in each st around. Join B.
Round 9: Alternate between dc and spike stitch around with no increases, e.g. 2dc then a spike, then 2dc on all similar rows.
Rounds 10–11: Dc in each st around.
Rounds 12–20: Rep Rounds 9–11 changing to a new colour every three rounds.
Round 21: Rep Round 9 with B.
Rounds 22–27: Dc in every st around. Do not fasten off.

Eyes (make two)

Using C, make a magic ring.
Round 1: 12dc into the ring. Join D.
Round 2: 2dc in each st around. [24 sts] Join E.
Round 3: (Dc in next dc, 2dc in next st) around. [36 sts]

Making up and finishing

Sew on the eyes. Using F, embroider the beak, working out from a central point to create the V shape.

Stuff the body, then using the attached B yarn, pinch the opening closed flat and dc across the top, catching stitches from both sides of the join. Fasten off and sew in end of yarn.

Ear tassels (optional)

Select long strands of the colours used in the body, double them over and using B, stitch over the middle to hold them in place. Wrap B around the strands a few times and pull tight to create a tassel. Fasten off and repeat on the other corner, trimming the tassels as short as you like.

Using B, sew a hanging loop at the top of the body, securing it in place with a few stitches.

• •

Red-breasted Robin

FINISHED
MEASUREMENTS

7cm (2¾ in) tall

YOU WILL NEED

Small quantities of Stylecraft Special DK yarn (100% Acrylic, 100g/295m per ball) in the following shades:

A Walnut

B Lipstick

C Cream

D Sunshine

Crochet hook: 3mm (UK 11) (US D3)

Yarn needle

Safety eyes

Scrap of yellow felt (optional)

Toy stuffing

Stitch marker

Start here

Body

Using A, make a magic ring
Round 1: 6dc into the ring.
Round 2: 2dc into each st around [12 sts]
Round 3: (Dc in next dc, 2dc in next st) around. [18 sts]
Round 4: (2dc, 2dc in next st) around [24 sts]
Round 5: (3dc, 2dc in next st) around [30 sts]
Rounds 6–9: Dc in each st around. Join B.
Round 10: Bldc in each st around.
Rounds 11–13: Dc in each st around.
Round 14: (4dc, 2dc in next st) around. [36 sts]
Round 15: (5dc, 2dc in next st) around. [42 sts]
Round 16: Dc in each st around. Join C.
Rounds 17–18: Dc in each st around.
Round 19: (5dc, dc2tog) around. [36 sts]
Round 20: (4dc, dc2tog) around. [30 sts]
Round 22: (3dc, dc2tog) around. [24 sts]
Place eyes at Round 11 and stuff. If you don't have safety eyes you can embroider them on with black yarn.
Round 23: (2dc, dc2tog) around. [18 sts]
Round 24: (Dc, dc2tog) around. [12 sts]
Round 25: Dc2tog around. [6 sts]
Fasten off. Add extra stuffing if needed before sewing closed. Embroider the beak or sew on a piece of felt.

Wings (make 2)

Using A, make a magic ring.
Round 1: 6dc into the ring.
Round 2: 2dc in each st around. [12 sts]
Rounds 3–9: Dc in each st around. Fasten off, leaving a long tail.

Making up and finishing

Using long tails, oversew the wings on either side of the body into the front loops left from Round 10 of the body. Make a hanging loop using A and secure with a few stitches.

• •

Scandi Gnome

FINISHED
MEASUREMENTS

16.5 cm (6½in) tall

YOU WILL NEED

Small quantities of Stylecraft Special DK yarn (100% Acrylic, 100g/295m per ball) in the following shades:

A Royal

B White

C Matador

D Soft peach

Crochet hook: 3mm (UK 11) (US D3)

Yarn needle

Toy stuffing

Stitch marker

Start here

Body

Using A, make a magic ring
Round 1: 6dc into the ring.
Round 2: 2dc into each dc. [12 sts]
Round 3: (Dc, 2dc in next st) around. [18 sts]
Round 4: (2dc, 2dc in next st) around. [24 sts]
Round 5: (3dc, 2dc in next st)

around. [30 sts]
Round 6: Bldc in each st around.
Rounds 7–14: Dc in each st around.
Round 15: (3dc, dc2tog) around.
[24dc]
Round 16: Dc in each st around.
Fasten off and sew in tail.

Beard

Cut strands of B and fold in half.
Insert the hook into one of the sts in
the last round worked, and pull the
yarn through. Pull the tails through
the loop to fix the strand in place.
Repeat along 6 more of the last round
of dc stitches. Untwist the ply of the
yarn and brush out to create the
beard. Trim into shape.

Hat

Using C, make a magic ring.
Round 1: 3dc into the ring.
Rounds 2–27: Dc in each st to last st,
2dc in last st. [finish with 30 sts]
Do not fasten off. Stuff.

Nose

Using D, make a magic ring.
Round 1: 8dc into the ring.
Rounds 2–3: Dc in each st around.
No need to stuff, just squash flat and
stitch in place.

Making up and finishing

Sew the nose in place on top of body
and over the top of the beard. Place
the hat above the body and turn the
gnome upside down. Using C still
attached, dc through both C and B
stitches around to join. Fasten off,
leaving a long tail and then pass the
C yarn through the hat, coming out
at the tip. Create a hanging loop and
secure with a few stitches.

• •

Woodland Toadstool

FINISHED
MEASUREMENTS

9cm (3½ in) tall

YOU WILL NEED

Small quantities of Stylecraft
Special DK yarn (100% Acrylic,
100g/295m per ball) in the
following shades:

A Lipstick

B Cream

Crochet hook: 3mm (UK 11)
(US D3)

Black embroidery cotton (floss)

Yarn needle

Safety eyes

Toy stuffing

Stitch marker

Start here

Cap

Using A, make a magic ring.
Round 1: 6dc into the ring.
Round 2: 2dc into each st around.
[12 sts]
Round 3: (Dc, 2dc in next st) around.
[18 sts]
Round 4: (2dc, 2dc in next st)
around. [24 sts]
Round 5: (3dc, 2dc in next st)
around. [30 sts]
Round 6: (4dc, 2dc in next st)
around. [36 sts]
Round 7: (5dc, 2dc in next st)
around. [42 sts]
Round 8: (6dc, 2dc in next st)
around. [48 sts]
Rounds 9–16: Dc in each st around.
Leave yarn attached.

Thread B onto yarn needle and
oversew several times in random
places around the outside of the cap
to create the spots.

Stalk and gills

Using B, make a magic ring.
Round 1: 6dc into the ring.
Round 2: 2dc into each st around.
[12 sts]
Round 3: (Dc, 2dc in next st) around.
[18 sts]
Round 4: (2dc, 2dc in next st)
around. [24 sts]
Round 5: (3dc, 2dc in next st)
around. [30 sts]
Round 6: (4dc, 2dc in next st)
around. [36 sts]
Rounds 7–13: Dc in each st around.
Round 14: (4dc, dc2tog) around.
[30 sts]
Round 15: Dc in each st around.
Round 16: Bldc in each st around.
Round 17: (4dc, 2dc in next st)
around. [36 sts]
Round 18: (5dc, 2dc in next st)
around. [42 sts]
Round 19: (6dc, 2dc in next st)
around. [48 sts]
Round 20: Dc in each st around.
Fasten off and weave in tail.

Making up and finishing

Place the safety eyes at Round 12 of
the stalk, about 7 dc apart. You can
also embroider the eyes if you prefer.
Stuff the stalk and place against the
cap WS to WS. Using A attached to
the cap, turn everything upside down
and dc around, working through both
sets of dc from the cap and the stalk,
to join together. About 10 stitches
from the end of the round, stuff the
cap to shape it correctly. Fasten off,
leaving a long tail.
Thread the tail onto a needle and
stitch through the top of the cap.
Create a hanging loop and secure in
place with a few stitches.
Using black embroidery cotton,
embroider the mouth.

Scandinavian Style

Designed by Jane Burns

Scandinavian Style never fails to please at Christmas, and this collection of easy-to-crochet baubles in classic red and white has real impact. Make as many as you like and add some handmade stocking bunting to complete the effect. These baubles look beautiful teamed with the other collections or just add dried scented orange rings and bundles of tied cinnamon sticks for an authentic Nordic look.

Scandinavian Style

Simple Scandinavian Baubles

FINISHED MEASUREMENTS

Each bauble: 20cm (8in) circumference

YOU WILL NEED

King Cole Merino Blend 4ply yarn(100% pure new wool, 50g/155mm per ball)

Select as appropriate for each bauble:

047 Aran

009 Scarlet

A 10g (¾oz) of 4ply main colour yarn

B Oddments of 4ply contrasting colour yarn

Crochet hook: 2.5mm (US B/1 or C/2)

Darning needle

Toy stuffing

Traditional Snowflakes

Pattern notes

The baubles are worked using the amigurumi principle, using only double crochet and working in a continuous spiral. The motif is applied afterwards using cross stitch.

Start here

Using A, start with a magic ring. Work 6dc into the ring and pull tail to close. Then continue working in a spiral.

Round 1: 2dc in each dc around. [12 sts]

Round 2: 2dc in next dc, 1dc around. [18 sts]

Round 3: 2dc in next dc, 2dc around. [24 sts]

Round 4: 2dc in next dc, 3dc around. [30 sts]

Round 5: 2dc in next dc, 4dc around. [36 sts]

Round 6: 2dc in next dc, 5dc around. [42 sts]

Round 7: 2dc in next dc, 6dc around. [48 sts]

Place marker (start of cross stitch chart).

Rounds 8–18: 1dc around.

Place marker (end of cross stitch chart).

Round 19: Dc2tog, 6dc around. [42 sts]

Round 20: Dc2tog, 5dc around. [36 sts]

Stuff the section just worked.

Round 21: Dc2tog, 4dc around. [30 sts]

Round 22: Dc2tog, 3dc around. [24 sts]

Round 23: Dc2tog, 2dc around. [18 sts]

Round 24: Dc2tog, 1dc around. [12 sts]

Round 25: Dc2tog around. [6 sts]

Add more stuffing and pull to close.

Making up and finishing

Darn in ends and using B, work the cross stitch motif in a contrasting colour, using the diagram as a guide. To make the hanging loop: using B ss into the top of the bauble. Ch24, then ss into first ch to make a loop and fasten off.

Love Heart

Follow the pattern for the Traditional Snowflake, using the cross stitch pattern to form your love heart in a contrasting colour.

Scandinavian Kisses

Follow the pattern for the Traditional Snowflake Baubles, adding evenly spaced single cross stitches all the way around the bauble.

Seasonal Stocking Bunting

FINISHED MEASUREMENTS

Each stocking: 12 x 7cm (4¾ x 2¾in)

YOU WILL NEED

King Cole Merino Blend 4ply yarn (100% pure new wool, 50g/155mm per ball)

Select as appropriate for each stocking:

046 Aran

009 Scarlet

A 10g (¾oz) of 4ply main colour yarn

B oddments of 4ply contrasting colour yarn

Crochet hook: 3mm (UK 11)

Darning needle

Pattern notes

The stockings are mainly worked using the amigurumi principle, using only double crochet and working in a continuous spiral, with the exception of the heel flap, which is worked flat. They start at the toe.

Start here

Using A, start with a magic ring. Work 6dc into the ring and pull tail to close. Then continue working in a spiral.

Round 1: 2dc in each dc around [12 sts]

Round 2: 2dc in next dc, 1dc around [18 sts]

Round 3: 2dc in next dc, 2dc around [24 sts]

Round 4: 2dc in next dc, 3dc around [30 sts]

Round 5–15: 1dc in each dc to end.

Heel flap

Round 1: Using B, work 15dc and turn.

Rounds 2–7: Ch1, 15dc, turn.

Leg

Join into the round and continue for the leg.

Round 1: Using A, work 7dc across the side edge of the heel flap, 15dc across instep, 8dc across second side edge of heel flap and join in the round. [30 sts]

Rounds 2–13: 1dc in each dc to end. [30 sts]

Change to B.

Rounds 14–17: 1dc in each dc to end. Do not fasten off.

Making up and finishing

To make a hanging loop, ch16, ss into base of ch16. Fasten off. Sew the back of the heel flap closed. Darn in ends and block. For the bunting cord, use the 3mm hook and cream yarn held double throughout, work a chain for desired length and fasten off. Darn in ends. Thread the stockings onto the cord.

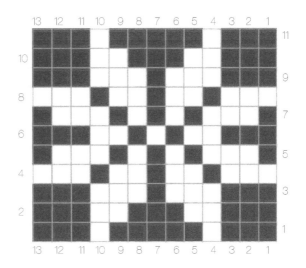

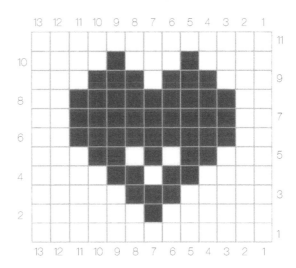

White Christmas

Designed by Lara Messer

The traditional at heart will adore the White Christmas collection, which includes mistletoe baubles in pastel shades, Chinese berry lanterns, white amigurumi Christmas trees, a chic cracker decoration and elegant snowflake bunting. The stylish designs look perfect teamed with glistening white fairy lights and classic glass baubles, either on a traditional tree or hanging from silver branches. Create your very own classic Christmas in crochet!

White Christmas

Mistletoe Bauble

Start here

Bauble

Using A and the 2.5mm crochet hook, make a magic ring.

Round 1: Ch3 (1tr) then 11tr into ring. Ss into initial ch3 to join. [12 sts]

Round 2: Ch3 (1tr) then 1tr in same st, 2tr in each st around. Ss into initial ch3 to join. [24 sts]

Round 3: Ch3 (1tr) then 1tr in same st, 1tr in next st, 2tr in next st around. Ss into initial ch3 to join. [36 sts]

Round 4: Ch3 (1tr) then 1tr in same st, 1tr in next 2 sts, 2tr in next st around. Ss into initial ch3 to join. [48 sts]

Cut yarn and sew in ends. When you complete the second circle, keep your yarn attached and use it to dc both circles together. When you have stitched three quarters of the way around, stuff the bauble, then continue dc around to close.

Ss into first dc, then ch60 to make the hanging loop and ss back into first dc. Fasten off and sew in ends.

Mistletoe

Using B and the 2mm crochet hook, ch14.

Starting in fifth ch from hook work 3ttr, 1dtr, 2tr, 2ht, 1dc, 1ss. Fasten off and leave a tail of yarn for sewing.

Making up and finishing

Using a darning needle, attach the mistletoe to the bauble using B. Do the same with the second leaf and then sew on two decorative pearls.

● ●

Chinese Berry Lantern

Start here

Using A and the 2.5mm crochet hook, crochet your rounds continuously – do not join with a ss.

Round 1: Ch2, 6dc in second chain from hook. [6 sts]

Round 2: 2dc in each st around. [12 sts]

Round 3: (2dc in next st, 1dc) 6 times. [18 sts]

Round 4: (2dc in next st, 2dc) 6 times. [24 sts]

Round 5: (2dc in next st, 3dc) 6 times. [30 sts]

Round 6: (2dc in next st, 4dc) 6 times. [36 sts]

Rounds 7–12: 1dc in each stitch around. [36 sts]

Round 13: (Dc2tog, 4dc) 6 times. [30 sts]

Round 14: (Dc2tog, 3dc) 6 times. [24 sts]

Round 15: (Dc2tog, 2dc) 6 times. [18 sts]

Stuff the lantern with toy stuffing.

Round 16: (Dc2tog, 1dc) 6 times. [12 sts]

Round 17: Dc2tog 6 times. [6 sts]

Cut yarn, leaving a long tail for attaching the top and bottom of your lantern. Sew around the top of the lantern and go through the body of the decoration to attach the base.

Lantern lid

Round 1: Using A, Ch2, 6dc in second ch from hook. [6 sts]

Round 2: 2dc in each st around. [12 sts]

Round 3: (2dc in next st, 1dc) 6 times. [18 sts]

Round 4: Blo 1dc in each st around. [18 sts]

Ss into next st, ch30 and ss directly across from the starting point to form a handle. Cut yarn and sew in ends.

Base

Round 1: Ch2, 6dc in second ch from hook. [6 sts]

Round 2: 2dc in each st around. [12 sts]

Round 3: (2dc in next st, 1dc)
6 times. [18 sts]
Round 4: Blo 1dc in each st around.
[18 sts]
Cut yarn and sew in ends.

For holly and berries

Using B, ch12.
Round 1: Using 2mm crochet hook,
1dc in second ch from hook, 1dc,
2htr, 2tr, 2dtr, 1tr, 1htr, 1dc, turn.
Now work on the other side of your
foundation chain:
1dc in the same ch as last dc, 1htr,
1tr, 2dtr, 2tr, 2htr, 2dc.

For pointed holly leaves

Round 2:
Ch1
1dc in the next st, ch2, ss in the top of
the dc you have just made, dc in the
same st, ss into the next 2 stitches.
1htr in the next st, ch2, ss into the top
of the htr you have just made, 1htr in
the same st, ss into the next 2 stitches.
1htr in the next st, ch2, ss into the top
of the htr you have just made, 1htr in
the same st, ss into the next 2 stitches.
1dc in the next st, ch 2, ss into the top
of the dc you have just made. Dc in
the same st and ss in the last st.
Turn to work on the other side.
1dc in the next st, ch2, ss in the top of
the dc you have just made, dc in the
same st, ss into the next 2 stitches.
1htr in the next st, ch2, ss into the top
of the htr you have just made, 1htr in
the same st, ss into the next 2 stitches.
1htr in the next st, ch2, ss into the
top of the htr you have just made,
1htr in the same st, ss into the next 2
stitches.
1dc in next st, ch 2, ss into the top
of the dc you have made, 1dc in the
same st.
Repeat one more time if you would
like your holly leaf to have another
point. Ss to end of leaf.
Ch12 (this is 1 ch sp which you later
use to attach your holly leaves to your
lantern, and ch12 for you to repeat
the pattern for another leaf).

For veins on the leaves

Insert hook into centre of leaf from
front to back. Pull yarn through and
work ss along centre of leaf.
Do not cut yarn. Repeat again to
make another, adjoining leaf – this
means you will not have ends to tidy
and the pair of leaves will look like
classic holly leaves joined together.

For berries

Using C, ch 2, dc in second chain
from hook.
Cut yarn and sew in ends with a
darning needle, helping your berry to
form a ball shape.

• •

White Christmas Tree

FINISHED
MEASUREMENTS

10cm (4in) tall

YOU WILL NEED

DMC Petra 3 yarn (100% cotton,
100g/280m per ball):

A 50g (1¾oz) of shade B5200
White

B Oddments of shade 54518
Light Blue

Oddments of DMC Light Effects
thread (100% polyester fibres) in

shade 5283 Silver

Crochet hooks: 2mm (UK 14),
2.5mm (US B/1 or C/2)

Small silver pearls (approx. 28)

Toy stuffing

Darning needle

Start here

Christmas tree

Using A and the 2.5mm crochet hook,
crochet the rounds continuously – do
not join.
Make a magic ring
Round 1: 6 dc in ring. [6 sts]
Round 2: 2dc in each st around.
[12 sts]
Round 3: Flo 1dc in each st around.
[12 sts]
Round 4: (Blo 1dc in next st, 2dc)
6 times. [18 sts]
Round 5: 1dc in each st around.
[18 sts]
Round 6: Flo 1dc in each st around.
[18 sts]
Round 7: (Blo 2dc, 2dc in next st).
[24 sts]
Round 8: 1dc in each st around.
[24 sts]
Round 9: Flo 1dc in each st around.
[24 sts]
Round 10: (Blo 3dc, 2dc in next st)
6 times. [30 sts]
Round 11: 1dc in each st around.
[30 sts]
Round 12: Flo 1dc in each st around.
[30 sts]
Round 13: (Blo 4dc, 2dc in next st)
6 times. [36 sts]
Round 14: 1dc in each st around.
[36 sts]
Round 15: Flo 1dc in each st around.
[36 sts]
Round 16: (Blo 5dc, 2dc in next st)
6 times. [42 sts]
Round 17: 1dc in each st around.
[42 sts]
Round 18: Flo 1dc in each st around.
[42 sts]
Round 19: (Blo 6dc, 2dc in next st)
6 times. [48 sts]
Round 20: 1dc in each st around.
[48 sts]
Round 21: Flo 1dc in each st around.
[48 sts]
Round 22: (Blo 7dc, 2dc in next st)
6 times. [54 sts]
Round 23: 1dc in each st around.
[54 sts]
Round 24: Flo 1dc in each st around.
[54 sts]

Round 25: (Blo 8dc, 2dc in next st) 6 times. [60 sts]
Round 26: 1dc in each st around. [60 sts]
Round 27: Flo 1dc in each st around. [60 sts]
Round 28: (Blo 9dc, 2dc in next st) 6 times. [66 sts]
Round 29: 1dc in each st around. [66 sts]
Cut yarn and sew in ends.

Christmas tree base

To crochet a circle the size of the bottom of your tree, first make a magic ring.
Round 1: 6dc in ring. [6 sts]
Round 2: 2dc in each st around. [12 sts]
Round 3: (2dc in next st, 1dc) 6 times. [18 sts]
Round 4: (2dc in next st, 2dc) 6 times. [24 sts]
Round 5: (2dc in next st, 3dc) 6 times. [30 sts]
Round 6: (2dc in next st, 4dc) 6 times. [36 sts]
Round 7: (2dc in next st, 5dc) 6 times. [42 sts]
Round 8: (2dc in next st, 6dc) 6 times. [48 sts]
Round 9: (2dc in next st, 7dc) 6 times. [54 sts]
Round 10: (2dc in next st, 8dc) 6 times. [60 sts]
Round 11: (2dc in next st, 9dc) 6 times. [66 sts]
Cut yarn and sew in ends.

Star

Using 2.5mm crochet hook and B, make a magic ring.
Ch1.
Round 1: (Dc into magic ring, ch3, dc in third chain from hook) 5 times. Pull tight. Cut yarn and sew in ends, leaving a long enough tail to attach your last star point to the first. Using white embroidery cotton and a needle, stitch the star to the top of the tree.

Tinsel

Use the 2.5mm crochet hook and two separate, continuous strands of C. Take one strand and thread through the pearls with the darning needle. Using the next strand, ss onto your hook and place both threads side by side.
Ch10 and pick up the first pearl by chaining over it.
Ch5 in-between each pearl and pick up pearls as you go. Continue to your desired length.
When finished, gently drape the tinsel around your tree and pin in place. Using white embroidery cotton and a needle, neatly stitch on your tinsel.

Making up and finishing

Stuff the tree with toy stuffing. Attach the bottom circle to the bottom of your tree by double crocheting all around. [66 sts]
To make the hanging loop, take 75cm (30in) of silver tapestry thread and, using a darning needle, go up through the bottom hole of the circle. Secure here to begin then push your needle straight up to one side of the star. Go back into the decoration at the opposite side of the star, making your loop the desired length. Secure invisibly within the tree. Cut yarn and tidy up any ends.

Christmas Cracker

FINISHED MEASUREMENTS

8cm (3¼in) long

YOU WILL NEED

DMC Petra 3 yarn (100% cotton, 100g/280m per ball):

A 30g (1oz) of Ecru

B Oddments of shade 53814 Jade

Oddments of DMC Light Effects thread (100% polyester fibres) in Gold.

Crochet hook: 2.5mm (US B/1 or C/2)

Card: 7cm x 3.5cm (2¾ x 1⅜in)

Toy stuffing

Darning Needle

Start here

Cracker

Using A, ch27 (foundation ch).
Row 1: 1tr into third chain from hook, 1tr into each st, turn.
Row 2: 1tr in each st.
Row 3: 1tr in each st.
Cut yarn and sew in ends. Ss to join the main body colour.
Row 4: Ch1 (1dc), 1dc in each st.
Rows 5–16: 1dc in each st, fasten off. Ss to join contrast colour.
Rows 17–19: Ch3 (1tr), 1tr in each st.
Row 20: To finish, work 1 row of dc to even out the opposite side's foundation row of ch27. Fasten off and sew in ends.

Star

Using A, make a magic ring.
Ch1.

Round 1: (Dc into magic ring, ch3, dc in third chain from hook) 5 times. Pull tight. Cut yarn and sew in ends, leaving a long enough tail to attach your last star point to the first. Using white embroidery cotton and a needle, stitch the star in place.

Making up and finishing

Stick the long sides of the card together to form a loose tube for the inside of the cracker.

Fold your crochet piece right sides together and, using a darning needle and corresponding yarn, whip stitch the cracker together. Slide your cardboard tube inside.

Stuff the inside of the tube with toy stuffing until full.

Using gold tapestry thread, make a bow at either end of the cracker and stitch in place using a needle and thread. Using the gold thread again, create a hanging loop at one end of the cracker, and secure in place with a couple of stitches.

Vintage Snowflake Bunting

FINISHED MEASUREMENTS

10cm (4in) each snowflake

YOU WILL NEED

DMC Petra 3 yarn (100% cotton, 100g/280m per ball):

A 50g (1¾oz) of shade B5200 White

B 50g (1¾oz) of shade 54518 Light Blue

C 50g (1¾oz) of shade 53024 Light Silver

Crochet hook: 2.5mm (US B/1 or C/2)

Darning needle

Start here

Round 1: Ch12 then ss to join in a ring.

Round 2: Ch1, 24dc into ring and ss into first dc to join. [24 sts]

Round 3: Ch1, 1dc in same st as ch1 *(1dc into next st, picot into this dc, 1dc into next st)*. Repeat from * around ending with picot then ss into then ss into first dc to join. You should have 12 picots and 12 spaces.

Round 4: Ch8, 1dtr in same st, ch4. *Miss the picot st, then 1dtr into dc between picots, ch4. Repeat from * around, ending with ch4, then ss into fourth ch of the first ch8 to join. [12 loops]

Round 5: Ch1, 5dc into ch4 loop of previous round. Repeat around and ss into first dc to join.

Round 6: Ch1, 1dc into blo of each of the first 5dc, ch15, miss next 5dc. Work Blo dc in each of the next 5dc.

Repeat around. Ss into first dc to join.

Round 7: Ch1, 1dc into blo of each of next 5dc (making sure you pick up the dc blo behind your ch1 as the first dc), then 15dc into your first ch15 loop. Repeat around. Ss into first dc to join.

Round 8: Ss into blo of next st, dc into next 3dc, miss 1dc, then go onto the loop section. Miss next dc then *(1dc into next 3dc, picot into third dc)* 4 times. 1dc into each of next 3dc, miss 1dc, then 1dc into blo of each of next 3dc. Miss 1dc, then rep from * to *, to end with 1dc in last 3dc. Miss 1dc. Repeat from * around. End with 1dc in last 3dc. Ss into first dc to join.

Cut yarn and sew in ends.
Spray starch liberally onto your finished snowflakes and apply a warm iron over them using a mesh or thin cloth.

Making up and finishing

Make the hanging loops for the bunting ends by repeating Rounds 1–3.

To make your snowflakes into a garland, use two balls of your chosen yarn colour. Use one ball and a darning needle to thread a loop through the top of your snowflakes and end pieces. Keep them threaded together and do not cut your yarn at this point.

Take your other ball of co-ordinating yarn and chain both yarns together for 50 chains. Pick up your first snowflake and chain tightly above your threaded loop. Chain 50 between each snowflake.

Cut yarn and sew in ends.

Santa's Grotto

Frozen Winter Wonderland

Fairy Tales

Scandinavian Style

White Christmas

Crochet Stitches

Abbreviations

blo: back loops only
bldc: back loop double crochet
blhtr: back loop half treble
ch: chain
ch-2 picot: ch2, ss in first of those ch
ch-3 picot: ch3, ss in first of those ch
dc: double crochet
dc2tog: double crochet two stitches together
dtr: double treble crochet
flo: front loops only
htr half treble crochet
picot: ch3, ss into top of dc you have just made (put your hook through v-shaped stitches)
rep: repeat
rs: right side
sk: skip
sp: space
ss: slip stitch
st/s: stitch/es
tr: treble crochet
ttr: triple treble crochet
ws: wrong side
yrh: yarn round hook

crochet terms

Be aware that crochet terms in the US are different from those in the UK. This can be confusing as the same terms are used to refer to different stitches under each system. The lists here give abbreviations and a translation of UK terms to US terms:

UK term	US term
single crochet	slip stitch
double crochet	single crochet
half treble	half double crochet
treble	double crochet
double treble	treble crochet
treble treble	double treble crochet

The starting loop or slipknot

Before you begin, you will need to make your first stitch. This will form the basis for all the following stitches.

Make a loop near the cut end of the yarn and insert the crochet hook into the loop, picking up the end of the yarn leading to the ball.

Draw this new loop of yarn through the existing loop, and gently pull on the end of the yarn leading to the ball to tighten this new loop around the hook. This is your first stitch.

Magic ring

The magic ring is an alternative way to begin crocheting in the round. In contrast to working into a chain or a chain circle, the basic magic ring allows you to tighten the first row, eliminating any opening.

To make a magic ring, make a loop a few inches from the end of your yarn. Grasp the join of the loop (where the two strands of yarn overlap) between your left thumb and forefinger. Insert hook into the loop from front to back. Draw up a loop. Ch 1 (does not count as st).

Insert hook into the loop, so you are crocheting over the loop and the yarn tail. Draw up a loop to begin your first sc of Round 1. Complete the sc. Continue to crochet over the loop and the yarn tail until you have the required number of sc for your first round. Grab the yarn tail and pull to draw the centre of the ring tightly closed. Begin your second round by crocheting into the first stitch of the first round.

Chain

(abbreviation = ch)
Almost all crochet items start with a length of chain stitches, and they also often appear within stitch patterns. Wherever the chain is required, it is made in the same way.

To make a chain stitch, take the yarn over the hook, wrapping it from the back, up over the hook towards the front, and then down and under the hook (every time the yarn is taken over the hook it should be done in this way). Now draw this new loop of yarn through the loop on the hook to complete the chain stitch.

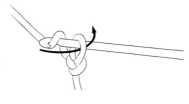

Double crochet

(abbreviation = dc)
A double crochet stitch is one of the most commonly used and easiest crochet stitches to make.

To make a double crochet, start by inserting the hook into the work at the required point. Take the yarn over the hook and draw this new loop of yarn through the loop on to the hook – there are now two loops on the hook.

Take the yarn over the hook again and draw this new loop through both the loops on the hook. This completes the double crochet stitch.

Treble crochet

(abbreviation = tr)
This is the other most commonly used crochet stitch: while a double crochet stitch is a very short, compact stitch, a treble stitch is taller and will add more height to the work.

To make a treble, wrap the yarn around the hook before inserting it into the work. Wrap the yarn around the hook again and draw this loop through the work – there are now three loops on the hook.

Wrap the yarn around the hook once more and draw this new loop through just the first two loops on the hook – the original loop and this new loop.

Wrap the yarn around the hook again and draw this new loop through both loops on the hook to complete the treble stitch.

Half treble

(abbreviation = htr)
A half treble stitch is a variation of a treble; its height is halfway between that of a double crochet and a treble stitch.

To make a half treble, start in exactly the way a treble is made until there are three loops on the hook. Wrap the yarn around the hook once more and draw this new loop through all three loops on the hook to complete the half treble stitch.

Back loop half treble

(abbreviation = blhtr)

This is a variation of the half treble stitch, working into the back loop only. To make a back loop half treble stitch, yarn over, insert the hook into the back loop only and pull up a loop. Yarn over and pull through all three loops to complete a stitch.

Slip stitch

(abbreviation = ss)

This stitch adds virtually no height to the work. It is generally used either to move the hook and working loop to a new point, or to join pieces.

To make a slip stitch, insert the hook into the work at the required point. Take the yarn over the hook and draw this new loop through both the work and the loop on the hook to complete the slip stitch.

Spike stitch

Spike stitches are stitches that extend down further than a crochet stitch typically would, to introduce extra colour, texture and interest into the design. Usually you would work your basic stitches into the tops of the stitches in the row or round below. With a spike stitch you might go two rows down or even further.

Crochet techniques

Joining new colours

When you're about to change colours, work until there are two loops left on your hook. Leaving a tail, draw the end of the new colour through the two loops on the hook.

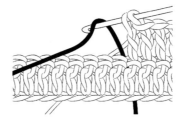

Continue in the pattern with the new ball of yarn. Once complete, weave in the tails of both colours to secure.

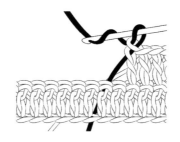

Working in the round

Sometimes, rather than working in rows, you will want to crochet in rounds.

When you begin, you will need to join the foundation chain to create a ring. Make the required number of chain stitches and then use a slip stitch into the first chain to join the work.

Then, with your first round, work either into the centre of the ring as if it were a chain space, or into the chain stitches themselves as normal.

At the end of the first round of any crochet piece, the first and last stitches need to be joined together to complete the circle. This is usually done by working a slipstitch into the top of the first stitch.

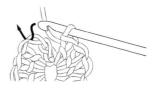

To make the second and every following round of crochet, the hook must, as when working in rows, be raised up to the height of the new stitches. So each new round of crochet will start with a turning chain.

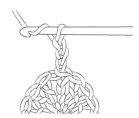

Fasten off

When you reach the end of your pattern, you will need to fasten off properly to ensure your crochet work is secure and does not unravel. This is very simple to do. You will finish with one loop on the hook. Cut the yarn, leaving a tail. Draw the tail through the loop on the hook and gently pull the yarn to tighten the stitch so that it does not unravel.

Sewing stitches

Backstitch

Blanket stitch

Cross stitch

French knot

1

2

3

Running stitch

Slip stitch

Whip stitch (oversewing)

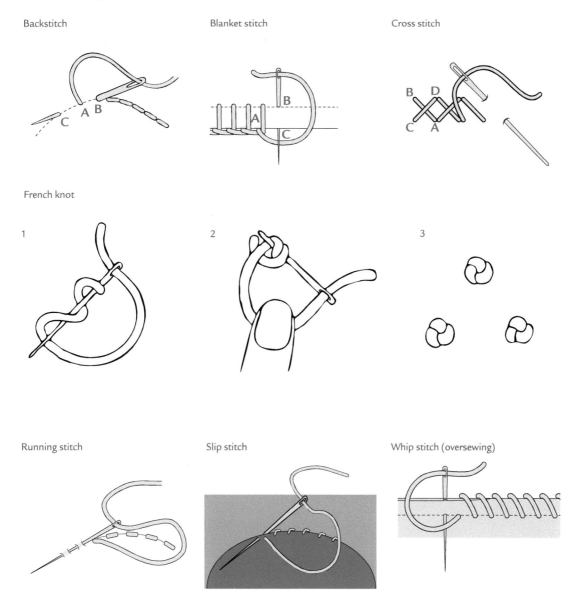

CONTRIBUTORS INDEX

Cara Medus
www.caramedus.com

Claire Wilson
www.claireabellemakes.com

Anna Fazakerley
www.dottydoily.com

Jane Burns
www.knittingimage.wordpress.com

Lara Messer
www.messyla.typepad.com

SUPPLIERS

Stitch Craft Create
www.stitchcraftcreate.co.uk

DMC Creative
www.dmccreative.co.uk
www.dmc-us.com

Stylecraft
www.stylecraft-yarns.co.uk

King Cole
www.kingcole.co.uk

A DAVID AND CHARLES BOOK
© David and Charles, Ltd 2014

David and Charles is an imprint of David and Charles, Ltd
Suite A, Tourism House, Pynes Hill, Exeter, EX2 5WS

Text and Designs ©David and Charles, Ltd 2014
Layout, Illustrations and Photography ©David and Charles, Ltd 2014

We have made every effort to ensure the accuracy of the contents of this
pattern booklet and cannot accept any liability for any errors.

A catalogue record for this book is available from the British Library.

ISBN-13 978-1-4463-0579-9 UK edition paperback

Printed in the UK through CPI Group (UK) Ltd for:
David and Charles, Ltd
Suite A, Tourism House, Pynes Hill, Exeter, EX2 5WS

David and Charles publishes high-quality books on a wide range of subjects.
For more information visit www.davidandcharles.com.